UNITED STATES

TAEKWON-DO FEDERATION

STEP-SPARRING HANDBOOK:

9TH GUP - WHITE BELT

through

2ND DAN - BLACK BELT

First Edition, August 1992.

Published in the United States of America
        by Lilley Gulch TKD

Printed in the United States of America
        by the United States Taekwon-Do Federation

Copyright © 1992 by C.E. Sereff and R.L. Mitchell

Library of Congress Catalogue Card Number 92-97105
ISBN 0-9622129-2-X

MASTER C.E. "CHUCK" SEREFF, EIGHTH DEGREE BLACK BELT
PRESIDENT OF THE UNITED STATES TAEKWON-DO FEDERATION

To the Students of the true art of Taekwon-Do:

This handbook is designed to act as a guide in developing your skill in step-sparring for rank testing within the United States Taekwon-Do Federation (U.S.T.F.). It is not intended, in any way, to replace your regular training under a qualified U.S.T.F. instructor. All aspects of these step-sparring guidelines should be reviewed with, and questions addressed to, a U.S.T.F. certified instructor. Quality instruction, and attention to the detailed requirements for each level of step sparring, will insure your understanding and quality compliance at each rank testing within the U.S.T.F.

Further information can be obtained from:

United States Taekwon-Do Federation
6801 W. 117th Ave. E-5
Broomfield, Colorado 80020
Phone: (303) 466-4963

A special thanks goes to Mr. Fred Akard, 5th Dan, and Mr. Rick Mitchell, 5th Dan, for their efforts in writing and producing the United States Taekwon-do Federation Step-Sparring Handbook.

Respectfully submitted,

Master C.E. Sereff, ITF, A-8-5
President,
United States Taekwon-Do Federation

TABLE OF CONTENTS

<u>Section</u>   <u>Page</u>

BASIC 3-STEP SPARRING - 9TH GUP HIGH WHITE BELT

Basic 3-Step Sparring

Basic 3-Step Sparring is performed alone, without a partner. Within the U.S.T.F., it is the required step-sparring format for promotion when testing for 9th Gup, High White Belt. This routine should performed in a formal manner with a high degree of discipline. When performing this level of step-sparring the student should keep the following points in mind:

- The student will perform both halves of Basic 3-Step Sparring without a partner. He/she will first perform the attackers portion, and then the defenders portion.
- It is important that all blocks are executed properly and with the proper tools.
- The student should use long stances.
- The student should not be in a hurry. Step-sparring is very sloppy when it is carried out in a fast motion.

Attacker Portion

Distance Measuring: The student will come to attention and then step forward with his/her right foot into a right walking stance.

Preparatory Move: The student steps back with his/her right foot while executing a left walking stance and a low block with the left outer forearm. The attacker should kihap at the same time as he/she executes the low block.

1

First Attack:

The student steps forward into a right walking stance while executing a right middle punch.

Second Attack:

The student steps forward into a left walking stance while executing a left middle punch.

Third Attack:

The student steps forward into a right walking stance while executing a right middle punch.

Return to
Ready Position:

The student steps backward into a parallel ready stance.

Defender Portion

Next Move:

The student kihaps to signal his/her readiness to begin the defender portion of this exercise.

First Defense:

The student steps back with the right foot into a left walking stance while executing a middle block with the left inner forearm. The interim hand position for this block is to the right of the body with both palms facing down, fists closed, and wrists touching with the left hand on the bottom. At the interim position, the hands at slightly lower than shoulder level.

Second Defense: The student steps back with the left foot into a right walking stance while executing a middle block with the right inner forearm. The interim hand position for this block is to the left of the body with both palms facing down, fists closed, and wrists touching with the right hand on the bottom. At the interim position, the hands at slightly lower than shoulder level.

Third Defense: The student steps back with the right foot into a left walking stance while executing a middle block with the left inner forearm. The interim hand position for this block is to the right of the body with both palms facing down, fists closed, and wrists touching with the left hand on the bottom. At the interim position, the hands at slightly lower than shoulder level.

Counter-Attack: Without stepping forward, changing stance, or leaning forward, the student executes a right middle punch and kihaps.

Return to
Ready Position: The student steps forward with his/her right foot into a parallel ready stance when given the command to return to the ready position.

BEGINNING 3-STEP SPARRING - 8TH GUP YELLOW BELT

Beginning 3-Step Sparring

Beginning 3-Step Sparring is performed with a partner. Within the U.S.T.F., it is the required step-sparring format for promotion when testing for 8th Gup, Low Yellow Belt. All Step-Sparring routines begin with a simple bow to your partner. The bow should be at 15°, while looking at your partner's eyes. The junior student should come up from the bow after their senior. All routines are to be performed in a formal manner with a high degree of discipline. At least one of the Beginning 3-Step Sparring routines performed at this level should use the same attacks, blocks, and counter-attacks as those used in Basic 3-Step Sparring. When performing this level of step-sparring the student should keep the following points in mind:

♦ It is important that all blocks are executed at the proper location and with proper tools.

♦ Since this beginning 3-step sparring, the student should make every effort to use correct stances and correct distance in order not to hurt each other.

♦ Distance and measurement are critical at this level of step-sparring.

♦ An appropriate block, attack, or counter-attack is a technique that is taught to the student at their belt level or a technique that is in one of the patterns up through their testing pattern.

♦ The Student should use long stances.

♦ The student should not be in a hurry. Step-sparring is very sloppy when it is carried out in a fast motion.

5

Number and Type of
Counter-Attack: Only one counter attack is to be used. It is to be a front kick or a hand technique that is taught to the student at their belt level. This includes all techniques used in patterns up through their testing pattern.

Distance Measuring: Both participants must come to attention. The attacker steps forward with his/her right foot into a right walking stance placing his/her right foot just to the outside the defender's left foot.

Preparatory Move: The attacker steps back with his/her right foot while executing a left walking stance and a low block with the left outer forearm. The attacker should kihap at the same time as he/she executes the low block.

Next Move: At the same time that the attacker steps back into a left walking stance, the defender moves the left foot to the left into a parallel ready stance. The Defender then kihaps to signal his/her readiness to begin.

First Attack: The attacker steps forward into a right walking stance placing his/her right foot to the outside of the defender's left foot while executing a right middle punch. The defender steps back with the right foot into a left walking stance while executing a middle block with the left inner forearm. The interim hand position for this block is to the right of the body with both palms facing down, fists closed, and wrists touching with the left hand on the bottom. At the Interim position, the hands at slightly lower than shoulder level. The block should LIGHTLY contact the attacker's wrist.

Second Attack: The attacker steps forward into a left walking stance placing his/her left foot to the inside of the defender's right foot while executing a left middle punch. The defender steps back with the left foot into a right walking stance while executing a middle block with the right inner forearm. The interim hand position for this block is to the left of the body with both palms facing down, fists closed, and wrists touching with the right hand on the bottom. At the Interim position, the hands at slightly lower than shoulder level. The block should LIGHTLY contact the attacker's wrist.

Third Attack:

The attacker steps forward into a right walking stance placing his/her right foot to the outside of the defender's left foot while executing a right middle punch. The defender steps back with the right foot into a left walking stance while executing a middle block with the left inner forearm. The interim hand position for this block is to the right of the body with both palms facing down, fists closed, and wrists touching with the left hand on the bottom. At the Interim position, the hands at slightly lower than shoulder level. The block should LIGHTLY contact the attacker's wrist.

Counter-Attack:

Without stepping forward, changing stance, or leaning forward, the defender executes an appropriate single counter-attack and kihaps. If the counter-attack is a Front Kick, the defender should then recover back to the original left walking stance. There is no need for the defender to attempt to make their counter-attack contact the attacker.

Return to
Ready Position:

Both the attacker and the defender step into a parallel ready stance, with the attacker stepping backward and the defender stepping forward. The attacker steps back to the ready position after the defender has initiated a forward movement to the ready position.

Preparation of the
Next Routine: If the distance between the participants needs to be
readjusted, the new attacker comes to attention.
This will signal the defender that measurement is
necessary.   The defender will then come to
attention.   The attacker steps forward with his/her
right foot into a right walking stance placing
his/her right foot just to the outside the defender's
left foot in order to recheck the distance.

INTERMEDIATE 3-STEP SPARRING - 7TH GUP YELLOW

Intermediate 3-Step Sparring

Within the U.S.T.F., Intermediate 3-Step is the required step-sparring format for promotion when testing for 7th Gup, High Yellow Belt. It should begin with a simple bow to your partner. The bow should be at 15°, while looking at your partner's eyes. The junior student should come up from the bow after their senior. All routines are to be performed in a formal manner with a high degree of discipline. When performing this level of step-sparring the student should keep the following points in mind:

♦ All blocks should be executed at the proper location and with the proper tools.

♦ Distance and measurement are important at this level of step-sparring.

♦ An appropriate block, attack, or counter-attack is a technique that is taught to the student at their belt level or a technique that is in one of the patterns up through their testing pattern. This is pattern Dan-Gun if the student is testing for 7th Gup, High Yellow Belt.

♦ The student should use good stances.

♦ The student should not be in a hurry. Step-sparring is very sloppy when it is carried out in a fast motion.

♦ If the attacker uses walking stances, and the defender uses walking stances: the attacker's foot positions are first to the outside of the defender's foot, then inside, and finally outside.

♦ If the attacker uses walking stances, and defender uses L-stances: all of the attacker's foot positions are to the outside of the defender's feet.

♦ If attacker uses L-stances, and the defender uses L-stances: the attacker's foot positions are first to the inside of the defender's foot, then outside, and finally inside.

♦ If attacker uses L-stances, and the defender uses walking stances: all of the attacker's foot positions will be inside of defender's feet.

Number and Type of
Counter-Attacks: Should include up to two counter-attacks. They are to be a foot-hand or a hand-foot technique combination. They may only consist of techniques that are taught to student at their belt level. This includes all required kicks up to and including the belt level of the student and all techniques used in patterns up through their testing pattern.

Distance Measuring: If the attacker is to start from a walking stance - Both students must come to attention. The attacker steps forward with his/her right foot into a right walking stance placing his/her right foot just to the outside the defender's left foot.

If the attacker is to start from an L-stance - Both students must come to attention. Attacker steps forward into left L-stance placing his/her right foot between the defender's feet.

Preparatory Move: If the attacker is to start from a walking Stance - The attacker steps back with his/her right foot while executing a left walking stance and a low block with the left outer forearm. The attacker should kihap at the same time as he/she executes the low block.

If the attacker is to start from an L-stance - The attacker steps back with his/her right foot into a right L-stance while executing a low block with the left outer forearm. The attacker should kihap at the same time as he/she executes the low block.

Next Move: At the same time that the attacker steps back into his/her preparatory stance, the defender moves the left foot to the left into a parallel ready stance. The Defender then kihaps to signal his/her readiness to begin.

First Attack: Attacker steps forward into the appropriate stance, placing their front foot on the correct side of the defender's foot, and executes the appropriate hand attack. Defender steps back with his/her right foot into an appropriate stance and executes an appropriate block. The block should LIGHTLY contact the correct portion of the attacker's attacking appendage.

Second Attack: Attacker steps forward with his/her rear leg into the appropriate stance, placing their front foot on the correct side of the defender's foot, and again executes the appropriate hand attack used in the first attack. Defender steps back into the same appropriate stance used in the first defence, but using the opposite leg, and executes the same appropriate block used in the first attack. The block should LIGHTLY contact the correct portion of the attacker's attacking appendage.

Third Attack: Attacker steps forward with his/her rear leg into the appropriate stance, placing their front foot on the correct side of the defender's foot, and executes the appropriate hand attack used in the first attack. Defender steps back into the same appropriate stance used in the first defence, but using the opposite leg, and executes the same appropriate block used in the first attack. The block should LIGHTLY contact the correct portion of the attacker's attacking appendage.

Counter-Attack: The defender executes up to two appropriate counter-attacks, and kihaps with his/her last punch or kick. The defender may move into another appropriate stance prior to, during, or at the end of the counter-attacking motion. If the counter-attack is a kick, the defender should step down with the kicking leg into an appropriate stance. There is no need for the defender to attempt to have their counter-attacks make more than light contact with the attacker.

Return to
Ready Position: Both the attacker and the defender step into a parallel ready stance, with the attacker stepping backward and the defender stepping forward. The attacker returns to a ready position after the defender has initiated a movement to return to the A-B line in a ready position.

Preparation of the
Next Routine: If the distance between the participants needs to be readjusted, the new attacker comes to attention. This will signal the defender that measurement is necessary. The defender will then come to attention. The attacker will then step forward to recheck the distance as it was done in the beginning of this step-sparring routine.

ADVANCED 3-STEP SPARRING - 6TH GUP GREEN BELT

Advanced 3-Step Sparring

Within the U.S.T.F., Advanced 3-Step is the required step-sparring format for promotion when testing for 6th Gup, Low Green Belt. It should begin with a simple bow to your partner. The bow should be at 15°, while looking at your partner's eyes. The junior student should come up from the bow after their senior. All routines are to be performed in a formal manner with a high degree of discipline. When performing this level of step-sparring the student should keep the following points in mind:

♦ It is important that all blocks are executed at the proper location and with proper tools.

♦ Distance and measurement are important at this level of step-sparring.

♦ The Student should use good stances.

♦ An appropriate block, attack, or counter-attack is a technique that is taught to the student at their belt level or a technique that is in one of the patterns up through their testing pattern. This is pattern Do-San if the student is testing for 6th Gup, Low Green Belt.

♦ The student should not be in a hurry. Step-sparring is very sloppy when it is carried out in a fast motion.

♦ If the attacker uses walking stances, and defender uses walking stances: the attacker's foot positions are first to the outside of the defender's foot, then inside, and finally outside.

♦ If the attacker uses walking stances, and defender uses L-stances: all of the attacker's foot positions are to the outside of the defender's feet.

- If attacker uses L-stances, and the defender uses L-stances: the attacker's foot positions are first to the inside of the defender's foot, then outside, and finally inside.
- If attacker uses L-stances, and the defender uses walking stances: all of the attacker's foot positions will be inside of defender's feet.

Number and Type of
Counter-Attacks: Should include up to three counter-attacks. These counter-attacks may consist of either a hand-foot-hand technique combination or a foot-hand-foot technique combination. These counter-attacks may only consist of techniques that are taught to the student at their belt level. This includes all required kicks up to and including the belt level of the student and all techniques used in patterns up through their testing pattern.

Distance Measuring: If the attacker is to start from a walking stance - Both students must come to attention. The attacker steps forward with his/her right foot into a right walking stance placing his/her right foot just to the outside the defender's left foot.

If the attacker is to start from an L-stance - Both students must come to attention. Attacker steps forward into either a right or left L-stance placing his/her lead foot between the defender's feet.

Preparatory Move: If the attacker is to start from a walking stance -
The attacker steps back with his/her right foot
while executing a left walking stance and a low
block with the left outer forearm. The attacker
should kihap at the same time as he/she executes
the low block.

If the attacker is to start from an L-stance - The
attacker steps back with his/her right foot into a
right L-stance while executing a low block with
the left outer forearm. The attacker should kihap
at the same time as he/she executes the low block.

Next Move: At the same time that the attacker steps back into
his/her preparatory stance, the defender moves the
left foot to the left into a parallel ready stance.
The Defender then kihaps to signal his/her
readiness to begin.

First Attack: Attacker steps forward into the appropriate stance,
placing their front foot on the correct side of the
defender's foot, and executes an appropriate hand
attack. Defender steps back with his/her right foot
into an appropriate stance and executes an
appropriate block. The block should LIGHTLY
contact the correct portion of the attacker's
attacking appendage.

Second Attack: Attacker steps forward with his/her rear leg into the appropriate stance, placing their front foot on the correct side of the defender's foot, and again executes the appropriate hand attack used in the first attack. Defender steps back into the same appropriate stance used in the first defence, but using the opposite leg, and executes the same appropriate block used in the first attack. The block should LIGHTLY contact the correct portion of the attacker's attacking appendage.

Third Attack: Attacker steps forward with his/her rear leg into the appropriate stance, placing their front foot on the correct side of the defender's foot, and executes the appropriate hand attack used in the first attack. Defender steps back into the same appropriate stance used in the first defence, but using the opposite leg, and executes the same appropriate block used in the first attack. The block should LIGHTLY contact the correct portion of the attacker's attacking appendage.

Counter-Attack: The defender executes up to three appropriate counter-attacks, and kihaps with his/her last punch or kick. The defender may move into another appropriate stance prior to, during, or at the end of the counter-attacking motion. If the counter-attack is a kick, the defender should step down with the kicking leg into an appropriate stance. There is no need for the defender to attempt to have their counter-attacks make more than light contact with the attacker.

Return to
Ready Position: Both the attacker and the defender step into a
                    parallel ready stance, with the attacker stepping
                    backward and the defender stepping forward. The
                    attacker returns to a ready position after the
                    defender has initiated a movement to return to the
                    A-B line in a ready position.

Preparation of the
Next Routine: It should not be necessary to adjust the distance
                    between the participants very often at this level.
                    However, if needed, the new attacker would come
                    to attention to signal the defender that a
                    measurement was necessary. The defender would
                    then come to attention. The attacker would then
                    step forward to recheck the distance as it was done
                    in the beginning of this step-sparring routine.

BEGINNING 2-STEP SPARRING - 5TH GUP GREEN BELT

Beginning 2-Step Sparring

Within the U.S.T.F., Beginning 2-Step is the required step-sparring format for promotion when testing for 5th Gup, High Green Belt. It should begin with a simple bow to your partner. The bow should be at 15°, while looking at your partner's eyes. The junior student should come up from the bow after their senior. All routines are to be performed in a formal manner with a high degree of discipline. When performing this level of step-sparring the student should keep the following points in mind:

♦ Students should be familiar with all terminology to insure that the step sparring routines proceed smoothly and there are no delays.

♦ Instructions given to sparring partners should be simple, clear, easily understood, and technically correct.

♦ It is important that all blocks are executed at the proper location and with proper tools.

♦ An appropriate block, attack, or counter-attack is a technique that is taught to the student at their belt level or a technique that is in one of the patterns up through their testing pattern. This is pattern Won-Hyo if the student is testing for 5th Gup, High Green Belt.

♦ Distance and measurement are no longer considered critical. At this level of step-sparring the student should have a good understanding of the concept of distance.

♦ The student should use good stances.

♦ The student should not be in a hurry. Step-sparring is very sloppy when it is carried out in a fast motion.

♦ Two-step sparring is not intended for the attacker to show off. The emphasis should be on the defender's performance.

23

Number and Type of
Counter-Attacks: Only one counter-attack is to be used, and it may be either a hand or a foot technique. (Double kicking techniques and 2-kick consecutive techniques will count as a single counter-attack.) This counter-attack may only consist of a technique that is taught to the student at their belt level. This includes all required kicks up to and including the belt level of the student and all techniques used in patterns up through their testing pattern.

Explanation of
Technique: Both the attacker and the defender step into a parallel ready stance, with the attacker stepping to the right and the defender stepping to the left. The defender will tell the attacker what stance to start the attack from and what attacks are to be executed by the attacker. These attacks will consist of either a combination foot-hand attack or a combination hand-foot attack.

Distance Measuring: Distance measurement is not considered critical at this level. However, if it is needed it should be conducted as follows: Both students must come to attention. Attacker steps forward into either a right or left L-stance placing his/her lead foot between the defender's feet.

Preparatory Move: The attacker will start from an L-stance. The attacker steps back with his/her foot into the appropriate L-stance and executes a middle guarding block with the forearm. The attacker should kihap at the same time as he/she executes the guarding block.

Next Move: The defender may start from either a parallel ready stance or from an L-stance. At the same time that the attacker steps back into his/her preparatory stance, the defender moves into the appropriate stance. The Defender then kihaps to signal his/her readiness to begin.

First Attack: Attacker executes the first of the prearranged sequence of attacks and the defender executes the first appropriate level defensive technique. Blocking techniques should LIGHTLY contact the correct portion of the attacker's attacking appendage.

Second Attack: Attacker executes the second of the prearranged sequence of attacks and the defender executes the second appropriate defensive technique. Blocking techniques should LIGHTLY contact the correct portion of the attacker's attacking appendage.

Counter-Attack: The defender executes a single appropriate counter-
                      attack, and kihaps. The defender may move into
                      another appropriate stance prior to, during, or at
                      the end of the counter-attacking motion. If the
                      counter-attack is a kick, the defender should step
                      down with the kicking leg into an appropriate
                      stance. There is no need for the defender to
                      attempt to have their counter-attacks make more
                      than light contact with the attacker.

Return to
Ready Position: Both the attacker and the defender step into
                      parallel ready stance, with the attacker stepping
                      forward and the defender stepping backward. The
                      attacker returns to a ready position after the
                      defender has initiated a movement to return to the
                      A-B line in a ready position.

INTERMEDIATE 2-STEP SPARRING - 4TH GUP BLUE BELT

Intermediate 2-Step Sparring

Within the U.S.T.F., Intermediate 2-Step is not a required step-sparring format. However, it is used as a training aid when preparing for the 4th Gup, Low Blue Belt Testing. It should begin with a simple bow to your partner. The bow should be at 15°, while looking at your partner's eyes. The junior student should come up from the bow after their senior. All routines are to be performed in a formal manner with a high degree of discipline. When performing this level of step-sparring the student should keep the following points in mind:

♦ Students should be familiar with all terminology to insure that the step sparring routines proceed smoothly and there are no delays.

♦ Instructions given to sparring partners should be simple, clear, easily understood, and technically correct.

♦ It is important that all blocks are executed at the proper location and with proper tools.

♦ An appropriate block, attack, or counter-attack is a technique that is taught to the student at their belt level or a technique that is in one of the patterns up through their testing pattern. This is pattern Yul-Gok if the student is testing for 4th Gup, Low Blue Belt.

♦ Distance and measurement are no longer considered critical. At this level of step-sparring the student should have a good understanding of the concept of distance.

♦ The student should use good stances.

♦ The student should not be in a hurry. Step-sparring is very sloppy when it is carried out in a fast motion.

♦ Two-step sparring is not intended for the attacker to show off. The emphasis should be on the defender's performance.

Number and Type of Counter-Attacks: Should include up to two counter-attacks. (Double kicking techniques and 2-kick consecutive techniques will count as a single counter-attack.) These counter-attacks may consist of either combination hand-foot or combination foot-hand techniques. These counter-attacks may only consist of techniques that are taught to the student at their belt level. This includes all required kicks up to and including the belt level of the student and all techniques used in patterns up through their testing pattern.

Explanation of Technique: Both the attacker and the defender step into a parallel ready stance, with the attacker stepping to the right and the defender stepping to the left. The defender will tell the attacker what stance to start the attack from and what attacks are to be executed by the attacker. These attacks will consist of either a combination foot-hand attack or a combination hand-foot attack.

Distance Measuring: Distance measurement is not considered critical at this level. However, if it is needed it should be conducted as follows: Both students must come to attention. Attacker steps forward into either a right or left L-stance placing his/her lead foot between the defender's feet.

Preparatory Move: The attacker will start from an L-stance. The attacker steps back with his/her foot into the appropriate L-stance and executes a middle guarding block with the forearm. The attacker should kihap at the same time as he/she executes the guarding block.

Next Move: The defender may start from either a parallel ready stance or from an L-stance. At the same time that the attacker steps back into his/her preparatory stance, the defender moves into the appropriate stance. The Defender then kihaps to signal his/her readiness to begin.

First Attack: Attacker executes the first of the prearranged sequence of attacks and the defender executes the first appropriate level defensive technique. Blocking techniques should LIGHTLY contact the correct portion of the attacker's attacking appendage.

Second Attack: Attacker executes the second of the prearranged sequence of attacks and the defender executes the second appropriate level defensive technique. Blocking techniques should LIGHTLY contact the correct portion of the attacker's attacking appendage.

Counter-Attack:

The defender executes up to two appropriate counter-attacks, and kihaps with his/her last punch or kick. The defender may move into another appropriate stance prior to, during, or at the end of the counter-attacking motion. If the last counter-attack is a kick, the defender should step down with the kicking leg into an appropriate stance. There is no need for the defender to attempt to have their counter-attacks make more than light contact with the attacker.

Return to
Ready Position:

Both the attacker and the defender step into parallel ready stance, with the attacker stepping forward and the defender stepping backward. The attacker returns to a ready position after the defender has initiated a movement to return to the A-B line in a ready position.

ADVANCED 2-STEP SPARRING - 4TH GUP BLUE BELT

Advanced 2-Step Sparring

Within the U.S.T.F., Advanced 2-Step is the required step-sparring format for promotion when testing for 4th Gup, Low Blue Belt. It should begin with a simple bow to your partner. The bow should be at 15°, while looking at your partner's eyes. The junior student should come up from the bow after their senior. All routines are to be performed in a formal manner with a high degree of discipline. When performing this level of step-sparring the student should keep the following points in mind:

♦ Students should be familiar with all terminology to insure that the step sparring routines proceed smoothly and there are no delays.

♦ Instructions given to sparring partners should be simple, clear, easily understood, and technically correct.

♦ It is important that all blocks are executed at the proper location and with proper tools.

♦ An appropriate block, attack, or counter-attack is a technique that is taught to the student at their belt level or a technique that is in one of the patterns up through their testing pattern. This is pattern Yul-Gok if the student is testing for 4th Gup, Low Blue Belt.

♦ Distance and measurement are no longer considered critical. At this level of step-sparring the student should have a good understanding of the concept of distance.

♦ The student should use good stances.

♦ The student should not be in a hurry. Step-sparring is very sloppy when it is carried out in a fast motion.

♦ Two-step sparring is not intended for the attacker to show off. The emphasis should be on the defender's performance.

Number and Type of
Counter-Attacks:
Should include up to three counter-attacks. (Double kicking techniques and 2-kick consecutive techniques will count as a single counter-attack.) These counter-attacks may consist of either combination foot-hand-foot or combination hand-foot-hand techniques. These counter-attacks may only consist of techniques that are taught to the student at their belt level. This includes all required kicks up to and including the belt level of the student and all techniques used in patterns up through their testing pattern.

Explanation of
Technique:
Both the attacker and the defender step into a parallel ready stance, with the attacker stepping to the right and the defender stepping to the left. The defender will tell the attacker what stance to start the attack from and what attacks are to be executed by the attacker. These attacks will consist of either a combination foot-hand attack or a combination hand-foot attack.

Distance Measuring:
Distance measurement is not considered critical at this level. However, if it is needed it should be conducted as follows: Both students must come to attention. Attacker steps forward into either a right or left L-stance placing his/her lead foot between the defender's feet.

Preparatory Move: The attacker will start from an L-stance. The attacker steps back with his/her foot into the appropriate L-stance and executes a middle guarding block with the forearm. The attacker should kihap at the same time as he/she executes the guarding block.

Next Move: Although the defender may start from either a parallel ready stance or from an L-stance, it is recommended that he/she start from a parallel ready stance at this level. At the same time that the attacker steps back into his/her preparatory stance, the defender moves into the appropriate stance. The Defender then kihaps to signal his/her readiness to begin.

First Attack: Attacker executes the first of the prearranged sequence of attacks and the defender executes the first appropriate level defensive technique. Blocking techniques should LIGHTLY contact the correct portion of the attacker's attacking appendage.

Second Attack: Attacker executes the second of the prearranged sequence of attacks and the defender executes the second appropriate level defensive technique. Blocking techniques should LIGHTLY contact the correct portion of the attacker's attacking appendage.

Counter-Attack: The defender executes up to three appropriate counter-attacks, and kihaps with his/her last punch or kick. The defender may move into another appropriate stance prior to, during, or at the end of the counter-attacking motion. If the last counter-attack is a kick, the defender should step down with the kicking leg into an appropriate stance. There is no need for the defender to attempt to have their counter-attacks make more than light contact with the attacker.

Return to
Ready Position: Both the attacker and the defender step into parallel ready stance, with the attacker stepping forward and the defender stepping backward. The attacker returns to a ready position after the defender has initiated a movement to return to the A-B line in a ready position.

BEGINNING 1-STEP SPARRING - 3RD GUP BLUE BELT

Beginning 1-Step Sparring

Within the U.S.T.F., Beginning 1-Step is the required step-sparring format for promotion when testing for 3rd Gup, High Blue Belt. It should begin with a simple bow to your partner. The bow should be at 15°, while looking at your partner's eyes. The junior student should come up from the bow after their senior. All routines are to be performed in a formal manner with a high degree of discipline. When performing this level of step-sparring the student should keep the following points in mind:

♦ Students should be familiar with all terminology to insure that the step sparring routines proceed smoothly and there are no delays.

♦ Instructions given to sparring partners should be simple, clear, easily understood, and technically correct.

♦ It is important that all blocks are executed at the proper location and with proper tools.

♦ It is important that the student demonstrates General Choi's idea of ending a conflict with "1 kick or 1 punch".

♦ An appropriate block, attack, or counter-attack is a technique that is taught to the student at their belt level or a technique that is in one of the patterns up through their testing pattern. This is pattern Joong-Gun if the student is testing for 3rd Gup, High Blue Belt.

♦ Distance and measurement are no longer considered critical. At this level of step-sparring the student should have a good understanding of the concept of distance.

♦ The student should use good stances.

♦ The student should not be in a hurry. Step-sparring is very sloppy when it is carried out in a fast motion.

♦ One-step sparring is not intended for the attacker to show off. The emphasis should be on the defender's performance.

Number and Type of
Counter-Attacks: Only one counter-attack is to be used, and it may be either a hand or a foot technique, but the student must use the other technique in the next routine. (Double or triple kicking techniques and 2- or 3-kick consecutive techniques will count as a single counter-attack.) This counter-attack may only consist of a technique that is taught to the student at their belt level. This includes all required kicks up to and including the belt level of the student and all techniques used in patterns up through their testing pattern.

Explanation of
Technique: Both the attacker and the defender step into a parallel ready stance, with the attacker stepping to the right and the defender stepping to the left. The defender will tell the attacker what stance to start the attack from and what attacks are to be executed by the attacker. These attacks will consist of either a single foot or a single hand attack.

Distance Measuring: Distance measurement is not considered critical at this level.

Preparatory Move:
If the attacker is to attack with a hand technique first, then he/she will start from a parallel ready stance. In this case, the attacker should kihap to signal his/her readiness to begin.

If the attacker is to attack with a kick first, then he/she will start from an L-stance. The attacker steps back with his/her foot into the appropriate L-stance and executes a middle guarding block with the forearm. The attacker should kihap at the same time as he/she executes the guarding block.

Next Move:
The defender has the choice to start from either a parallel ready stance, or an L-stance. At the same time that the attacker steps back into his/her preparatory stance, the defender moves into his/her chosen beginning stance. The Defender then kihaps to signal his/her readiness to begin.

Attack:
Attacker executes the prearranged attack and the defender executes the an appropriate level defensive technique. Blocking techniques should LIGHTLY contact the correct portion of the attacker's attacking appendage.

37

Counter-Attack: The defender executes a single appropriate counter-attack. The defender may move into another appropriate stance prior to, during, or at the end of the counter-attacking motion. After the counter-attack, the defender steps back into an L-stance, executes a middle guarding block, and kihaps. However, if the counter-attack is a kick, the defender should first step down with the kicking leg into an appropriate stance, then move his/her front foot back into an L-stance, execute a middle guarding block, and kihap. There is no need for the defender to attempt to have their counter-attacks make more than light contact with the attacker.

Return to
Ready Position: Both the attacker and the defender step into parallel ready stance, with the attacker stepping forward and the defender stepping backward. The attacker returns to a ready position after the defender has initiated a movement to return to the A-B line in a ready position.

INTERMEDIATE 1-STEP SPARRING - 2ND GUP RED BELT

Intermediate 1-Step Sparring

Within the U.S.T.F., Intermediate 1-Step is the required step-sparring format for promotion when testing for 2nd Gup, Low Red Belt. It should begin with a simple bow to your partner. The bow should be at 15°, while looking at your partner's eyes. The junior student should come up from the bow after their senior. All routines are to be performed in a formal manner with a high degree of discipline. When performing this level of step-sparring the student should keep the following points in mind:

♦ Students should be familiar with all terminology to insure that the step sparring routines proceed smoothly and there are no delays.

♦ Instructions given to sparring partners should be simple, clear, easily understood, and technically correct.

♦ It is important that all blocks are executed at the proper location and with proper tools.

♦ It is important that the student demonstrate General Choi's idea that any of the techniques used are capable of ending a conflict with "1 kick or 1 punch".

♦ An appropriate block, attack, or counter-attack is a technique that is taught to the student at their belt level or a technique that is in one of the patterns up through their testing pattern. This is pattern Toi-Gye if the student is testing for 2nd Gup, Low Red Belt.

♦ Distance and measurement are no longer considered critical. At this level of step-sparring the student should have a good understanding of the concept of distance.

♦ The student should use good stances.

- The student should not be in a hurry. Step-sparring is very sloppy when it is carried out in a fast motion.
- One-step sparring is not intended for the attacker to show off. The emphasis should be on the defender's performance.

Number and Type of
Counter-Attacks: Should include up to two counter-attacks. They may consist of either combination hand-foot or combination foot-hand techniques. (Double or triple kicking techniques and 2- or 3-kick consecutive techniques will count as a single counter-attack.) These counter-attacks may only consist of techniques that are taught to the student at their belt level. This includes all required kicks up to and including the belt level of the student and all techniques used in patterns up through their testing pattern.

Explanation of
Technique: Both the attacker and the defender step into a parallel ready stance, with the attacker stepping to the right and the defender stepping to the left. The defender will tell the attacker what stance to start the attack from and what attacks are to be executed by the attacker. These attacks will consist of either a single foot or a single hand attack.

Distance Measuring: Distance measurement is not considered critical at this level.

Preparatory Move: If the attacker is to attack with a hand technique first, then he/she will start from a parallel ready stance. In this case, the attacker should kihap to signal his/her readiness to begin.

If the attacker is to attack with a kick, then he/she starts from an L-stance.

In the case of the parallel ready stance the attacker should kihap to signal his/her readiness to begin.

In the case of the L-stance the attacker steps back with his/her foot into the appropriate L-stance and executes a middle guarding block with the forearm. The attacker should kihap at the same time as he/she executes the guarding block.

Next Move: The defender has the choice to start from either a parallel ready stance, or an L-stance. At the same time that the attacker steps back into his/her preparatory stance, the defender moves into his/her chosen beginning stance. The Defender then kihaps to signal his/her readiness to begin.

Attack: Attacker executes the prearranged attack and the defender executes the first appropriate level defensive technique. Blocking techniques should LIGHTLY contact the correct portion of the attacker's attacking appendage.

Counter-Attack: The defender executes up to two appropriate
                    counter-attacks. The defender may move into
                    another appropriate stance prior to, during, or at
                    the end of the counter-attacking motion. After the
                    last counter-attack, the defender steps back with
                    his/her front foot into an L-stance, executes a
                    middle guarding block, and kihaps. However, if
                    the counter-attack is a kick, the defender should
                    first step down with the kicking leg into an
                    appropriate stance, then move his/her front foot
                    back into an L-stance, execute a middle guarding
                    block, and kihap. There is no need for the
                    defender to attempt to have their counter-attacks
                    make more than light contact with the attacker.

Return to
Ready Position: Both the attacker and the defender step into
                    parallel ready stance, with the attacker stepping
                    forward and the defender stepping backward. The
                    attacker returns to a ready position after the
                    defender has initiated a movement to return to the
                    A-B line in a ready position.

ADVANCED 1-STEP SPARRING - 1ST GUP RED BELT

Advanced 1-Step Sparring

Within the U.S.T.F., Advanced 1-Step is one of the two required step-sparring formats for promotion when testing for 1st Gup, High Red Belt. It should begin with a simple bow to your partner. The bow should be at 15°, while looking at your partner's eyes. The junior student should come up from the bow after their senior. All routines are to be performed in a formal manner with a high degree of discipline. When performing this level of step-sparring the student should keep the following points in mind:

◆ Students should be familiar with all terminology to insure that the step sparring routines proceed smoothly and there are no delays.

◆ Instructions given to sparring partners should be simple, clear, easily understood, and technically correct.

◆ It is important that all blocks are executed at the proper location and with proper tools.

◆ It is important that the student demonstrate General Choi's idea that any of the techniques used are capable of ending a conflict with "1 kick or 1 punch".

◆ Now is the time for the student to show off his/her "hot-dog" kicks.

◆ An appropriate block, attack, or counter-attack is a technique that is taught to the student at their belt level or a technique that is in one of the patterns up through their testing pattern. This is pattern Hwa-Rang if the student is testing for 1st Gup, High Red Belt.

◆ Distance and measurement are no longer considered critical. At this level of step-sparring the student should have a good understanding of the concept of distance.

- The student should use good stances.
- The student should not be in a hurry. Step-sparring is very sloppy when it is carried out in a fast motion.
- One-step sparring is not intended for the attacker to show off. The emphasis should be on the defender's performance.

Number and Type of
Counter-Attacks: Multiple counter-attacks are to be used. These counter-attacks may consist of combination and consecutive techniques with hands and/or feet, but the number of counter-attacks should not be excessive. These counter-attacks may only consist of techniques that are taught to the student at their belt level. This includes all required kicks up to and including the belt level of the student and all techniques used in patterns up through their testing pattern.

Explanation of
Technique: Both the attacker and the defender step into a parallel ready stance, with the attacker stepping to the right and the defender stepping to the left. The defender will tell the attacker what stance to start the attack from and what attacks are to be executed by the attacker. These attacks will consist of either a single foot or a single hand attack.

Distance Measuring: Distance measurement is not considered critical at this level.

44

Preparatory Move: If the attacker is to attack with a hand technique first, then he/she will start from a parallel ready stance. In this case, the attacker should kihap to signal his/her readiness to begin.

If the attacker is to attack with a kick, then he/she starts from an L-stance.

In the case of the parallel ready stance the attacker should kihap to signal his/her readiness to begin.

In the case of the L-stance the attacker steps back with his/her foot into the appropriate L-stance and executes a middle guarding block with the forearm. The attacker should kihap at the same time as he/she executes the guarding block.

Next Move: The defender has the choice to start from either a parallel ready stance, or an L-stance. At the same time that the attacker steps back into his/her preparatory stance, the defender moves into his/her chosen beginning stance. The Defender then kihaps to signal his/her readiness to begin.

Attack: Attacker executes the prearranged attack and the defender executes an appropriate level defensive technique. Blocking techniques should LIGHTLY contact the correct portion of the attacker's attacking appendage.

Counter-Attack: The defender executes multiple appropriate counter-attacks. The defender may move into another appropriate stance prior to, during, or at the end of the counter-attacking motion. After the last counter-attack, the defender steps back with his/her front foot into an L-stance, executes a middle guarding block, and kihaps. However, if the counter-attack is a kick, the defender should first step down with the kicking leg into an appropriate stance, then move his/her front foot back into an L-stance, execute a middle guarding block, and kihap. There is no need for the defender to attempt to have their counter-attacks make more than light contact with the attacker.

Return to
Ready Position: Both the attacker and the defender step into parallel ready stance, with the attacker stepping forward and the defender stepping backward. The attacker returns to a ready position after the defender has initiated a movement to return to the A-B line in a ready position.

BEGINNING SEMI-FREE SPARRING - 1ST GUP RED BELT

Beginning Semi-Free Step Sparring

Within the U.S.T.F., Beginning Semi-Free is one of the required step-sparring formats for promotion when testing for 1st Gup, High Red Belt. It should begin with a simple bow to your partner. The bow should be at 15°, while looking at your partner's eyes. The junior student should come up from the bow after their senior. All routines are to be performed in a formal manner with a high degree of discipline. When performing this level of step-sparring the student should keep the following points in mind:

- It is important that all blocks are executed at the proper location and with proper tools.
- An appropriate block, attack, or counter-attack is a technique that is taught to the student at their belt level or a technique that is in one of the patterns up through their testing pattern. This is pattern Hwa-Rang if the student is testing for 1st Gup, High Red Belt.
- It is important that the student demonstrate General Choi's idea that any of the techniques used are capable of ending a conflict with "1 kick or 1 punch".
- Distance and measurement are no longer considered critical. At this level of step-sparring the student should have a good understanding of the concept of distance.
- The student should use good stances.
- The student should not be in a hurry. Step-sparring is very sloppy when it is carried out in a fast motion.

Number of
Counters: There are two attacks/counter-attacks executed by
                             each participant.   The initial attacker's two
                             attacking moves are to be either a foot/hand, or
                             hand/foot set of techniques.   Defender must
                             counter with the same class of counter-attack as
                             that used by the attacker. (i.e. a foot attack to
                             answer a foot attack, and a hand attack to answer
                             a hand attack.) If attacker executes a flying attack
                             technique, then the defender must execute a flying
                             block and answer with a flying attack.   These
                             attacks and counter-attacks may only consist of
                             techniques that are taught to the student at their
                             belt level. This includes all required kicks up to
                             and including the belt level of the student and all
                             techniques used in patterns up through their testing
                             pattern.

Preparatory Move: Both the attacker and the defender step into a
                             parallel ready stance, with the attacker stepping to
                             the right and the defender stepping to the left.

Next Move: Both the attacker and the defender step back into
                             an L-stance. The attacker then kihaps to signal
                             his/her intention to execute the first attack.

First Attack: Attacker executes an appropriate hand or foot
                             attack. The defender will simultaneously execute
                             an appropriate block. Blocking techniques should
                             LIGHTLY contact the correct portion of the
                             attacker's attacking appendage.

First
Counter-Attack:
The original defender executes an appropriate hand or foot counter-attack. The original attacker will simultaneously execute an appropriate Block. Blocking techniques should LIGHTLY contact the correct portion of the attacker's attacking appendage.

Second Attack:
The original attacker executes an appropriate hand or foot attack. The original defender will simultaneously either execute an appropriate Block. Blocking techniques should LIGHTLY contact the correct portion of the attacker's attacking appendage.

Final
Counter-Attack:
The original defender executes an appropriate hand or foot counter-attack. It is not necessary for the original attacker to block the last counter-attack. There is also no need for the defender to attempt to have their counter-attack make more than light contact with the attacker.

Next Move:
After the original defender has completed his/her last counter-attack, both the original defender and the original attacker step back into an L-stance, execute a middle guarding block, and the original defender kihaps. However, if the counter-attack is a kick, the defender should first step down with the kicking leg into an appropriate stance, then both the original defender and the original attacker step back into an L-stance, execute a middle guarding block, and the original defender kihaps.

Return to
Ready Position: Both the original defender and the original attacker
step forward into parallel ready stances.   The
attacker returns to a ready position after the
defender has initiated a movement to return to the
A-B line in a ready position.

ADVANCED SEMI-FREE SPARRING - 1ST DAN BLACK BELT

Advanced Semi-Free Step Sparring

Within the U.S.T.F., Advanced Semi-Free is the required step-sparring format for promotion when testing for 1st Dan, Black Belt. It should begin with a simple bow to your partner. The bow should be at 15°, while looking at your partner's eyes. The junior student should come up from the bow after their senior. All routines are to be performed in a formal manner with a high degree of discipline. When performing this level of step-sparring the student should keep the following points in mind:

♦ It is important that all blocks are executed at the proper location and with proper tools.

♦ An appropriate block, attack, or counter-attack is a technique that is taught to the student at their belt level or a technique that is in one of the patterns up through their testing pattern. This is pattern Choong-Moo if the student is testing for 1st Dan, Black Belt.

♦ It is important that the student demonstrate General Choi's idea that any of the techniques used are capable of ending a conflict with "1 kick or 1 punch".

♦ Distance and measurement are no longer considered critical. At this level of step-sparring the student should have a good understanding of the concept of distance.

♦ The student should use good stances.

♦ The student should not be in a hurry. Step-sparring is very sloppy when it is carried out in a fast motion.

Number of
Counters: There are three attacks/counter-attacks executed by each participant. The initial attacker's three attacking moves are to be either a foot/hand/foot, or a hand/foot/hand set of techniques. The defender must counter each attack with the same class of counter-attack as that used by the attacker. (i.e. a foot attack to answer a foot attack, and a hand attack to answer a hand attack.) If the attacker executes a flying attack technique, then the defender must execute a flying block and answer with a flying attack. These attacks and counter-attacks may only consist of techniques that are taught to the student at their belt level. This includes all required kicks up to and including the belt level of the student and all techniques used in patterns up through their testing pattern.

Preparatory Move: Both the attacker and the defender step into a parallel ready stance, with the attacker stepping to the right and the defender stepping to the left.

Next Move: Both the attacker and the defender step back into an L-stance. The attacker then kihaps to signal his/her intention to execute the first attack.

First Attack: Attacker executes an appropriate hand or foot attack. The defender will simultaneously execute an appropriate block. Blocking techniques should LIGHTLY contact the correct portion of the attacker's attacking appendage.

First
Counter-Attack: The original defender executes an appropriate hand or foot counter-attack. The original attacker will simultaneously execute an appropriate Block. Blocking techniques should LIGHTLY contact the correct portion of the attacker's attacking appendage.

Second Attack: The original attacker executes an appropriate hand or foot attack. The original defender will simultaneously execute an appropriate Block. Blocking techniques should LIGHTLY contact the correct portion of the attacker's attacking appendage.

Second
Counter-Attack: The original defender executes an appropriate hand or foot counter-attack. The original attacker will simultaneously execute an appropriate Block. Blocking techniques should LIGHTLY contact the correct portion of the attacker's attacking appendage.

Third Attack: The original attacker executes an appropriate hand or foot attack. The original defender will simultaneously execute an appropriate Block. Blocking techniques should LIGHTLY contact the correct portion of the attacker's attacking appendage.

Final
Counter-Attack: The original defender executes an appropriate hand
or foot counter-attack. It is not necessary for the
original attacker to block the last counter-attack.
There is also no need for the defender to attempt
to have their counter-attack make more than light
contact with the attacker.

Next Move: After the original defender has completed his/her
last counter-attack, both the original defender and
the original attacker step back into an L-stance,
execute a middle guarding block, and the original
defender kihaps. However, if the counter-attack is
a kick, the defender should first step down with
the kicking leg into an appropriate stance, then
both the original defender and the original attacker
step back into an L-stance, execute a middle
guarding block, and the original defender kihaps.

Return to
Ready Position: Both the original defender and the original attacker
step forward into parallel ready stances. The
attacker returns to a ready position after the
defender has initiated a movement to return to the
A-B line in a ready position.

MODEL SPARRING - 2ND DAN BLACK BELT

Model Step Sparring

Within the U.S.T.F., Model Sparring is the required step-sparring format for promotion when testing for 2nd Dan, Black Belt. It should begin with a simple bow to your partner. The bow should be at 15°, while looking at your partner's eyes. The junior student should come up from the bow after their senior. All routines are to be performed in a formal manner with a high degree of discipline. When performing this level of step-sparring the student should keep the following points in mind:

♦ Students should be familiar with all terminology to insure that the step sparring routines proceed smoothly and there are no delays.

♦ Instructions given to sparring partners should be simple, clear, easily understood, and technically correct.

♦ It is important that all blocks are executed at the proper location and with proper tools.

♦ It is important that the student demonstrate General Choi's idea that any of the techniques used are capable of ending a conflict with "1 kick or 1 punch".

♦ Model Sparring is designed for the student to show off his/her high, "posed", and "hot-dog" kicks as well as difficult combination and consecutive kicking combinations.

♦ An appropriate block, attack, or counter-attack is a technique that is taught to the student at their belt level or a technique that is in one of the patterns up through their testing patterns. These are patterns Kwang-Gye, Gae-Beck, and Po-Eun if the student is testing for 2nd Dan, Black Belt.

♦ Distance and measurement are not considered critical. At this level of step-sparring the student should have a very good understanding of the concept of distance.

♦ The student should use good stances.

♦ The student should not be in a hurry. Step-sparring is very sloppy when it is carried out in a fast motion.

Number and Type of
Counter-Attacks: Multiple counter-attacks are to be used. These counter-attacks may only consist of techniques that are taught to the student at their belt level. This includes all required kicks up to and including the belt level of the student and all techniques used in patterns up through their testing pattern.

Explanation of
Technique: Both the attacker and the defender step into a parallel ready stance, with the attacker stepping to the right and the defender stepping to the left. The defender will tell the attacker what stance to start the attack from and what attack is to be executed by the attacker. This attack will consist of either a single foot or a single hand attack.

Distance Measuring: Distance measurement is not considered critical at this level.

Preparatory Move: If the attacker is to attack with a hand technique first, then he/she will start from a parallel ready stance. In this case, the attacker should kihap to signal his/her readiness to begin.

If the attacker is to attack with a kick first, then he/she will start from an L-stance. The attacker steps back with his/her foot into the appropriate L-stance and executes a middle guarding block with the forearm. The attacker should kihap at the same time as he/she executes the guarding block.

Next Move: The defender has the choice to start from either a parallel ready stance, or an L-stance. At the same time that the attacker steps back into his/her preparatory stance, the defender moves into his/her chosen beginning stance. The Defender then kihaps to signal his/her readiness to begin.

Attack: Attacker executes the prearranged attack and the defender executes an appropriate level defensive technique. Blocking techniques should LIGHTLY contact the correct portion of the attacker's attacking appendage.

Fast
Counter-Attacks: The defender executes multiple appropriate counter-attacks (primarily foot techniques). The defender may move into another appropriate stance prior to, during, or at the end of the counter-attacking motions. After the last counter-attack, the defender steps back with his/her front foot into an L-stance, executes a middle guarding block, and kihaps. However, if the counter-attack is a kick, the defender should first step down with the kicking leg into an appropriate stance, then move his/her front foot back into an L-stance, execute a middle guarding block, and kihap. There is no need for the defender to attempt to have their counter-attacks make more than light contact with the attacker.

Return to
Ready Position: Both the attacker and the defender step into parallel ready stance, with the attacker stepping forward and the defender stepping backward. The attacker returns to a ready position after the defender has initiated a movement to return to the A-B line in a ready position.

Next Move: The defender returns to the defensive stance used prior to the "Fast Attack." At the same time, the defender also moves into the stance he/she used prior to the "Fast Attack." The defender then kihaps to signal his/her readiness to begin.

Slow Attack: The attacker executes the same attack as used previously in the "Fast Attack" but executes it as a slow motion technique.

Slow
Counter-Attacks: The defender executes the same multiple appropriate counter-attacks as used previously in the "Fast Counter-Attacks" but executed as slow motion techniques. After the last counter-attack, the defender steps back with his/her front foot into an L-stance, executes a middle guarding block, and kihaps. However, if the counter-attack is a kick, the defender should first step down with the kicking leg into an appropriate stance, then move his/her front foot back into an L-stance, execute a middle guarding block, and kihap.

Return to
Ready Position: Both the attacker and the defender step into parallel ready stance, with the attacker stepping forward and the defender stepping backward. The attacker returns to a ready position after the defender has initiated a movement to return to the A-B line in a ready position.

NOTES

NOTES

NOTES

NOTES